D1473901

Gift of the Unicorn

Gift of the Unicorn

The Story of Lue Gim Gong, Florida's Citrus Wizard

VIRGINIA ARONSON

Pineapple Press, Inc.
Sarasota, Florida

Inquiries should be addressed to:

Pineapple Press, Inc.
P.O. Box 3889
Sarasota, Florida 34230

www.pineapplepress.com

Poem on page 7 from *Chinese Love Lyrics,* copyright © 1964, Peter Pauper Press. Reprinted by permission.

Poem on page 71 from *Cold Mountain: 100 Poems by the T'ang Poet Han-shan,* edited by Burton Watson, copyright © 1970, Columbia University Press. Reprinted by permission of the publisher.

Photos on pages 54–55 and 70 are reproduced courtesy of the Florida State Archives. Cover photo and all others in text are reproduced courtesy of the West Volusia Historical Society.

Chinese lettering created by Language Exchange International (www. LanguageExchange.com).

LIBRARY OF CONGRESS CATALOGING-IN-PUBLICATION DATA

Aronson, Virginia.
      Gift of the unicorn : the story of Lue Gim Gong, Florida's citrus wizard / Virginia Aronson.—1st ed.
         p.   cm.
    Includes bibliographical references.
    ISBN 1-56164-264-9 (hb : alk. paper)
      1. Lue, Gim Gong, 1858 or 9–1925. 2. Horticulturists—Florida—De Land—Biography.   3.   Fruit   growers—Florida—De   Land—Biography. 4. Oranges—Florida—De Land—History. 5. Citrus—Florida—De Land—History. I. Title.

SB63.L78 A76 2002
634'.092—dc21
  [B]
                                                               200202534

First Edition
10 9 8 7 6 5 4 3 2 1

Design by Carol Tornatore
Printed in the United States of America

To the spirit of Lue Gim Gong

double brilliance (Lue Gim Gong)

If I were a tree or a plant
I would feel the soft influence of spring.
Since I am a man. . . .
Do not be astonished at my joy.

—Anonymous (A.D. 1005)

There is an ancient folktale still told in China called "Gift of the Unicorn." The Chinese people once believed in the *Ki-lin*, a magical creature that looked like a pale, miniature horse with a single pearly horn in the center of its forehead. The *Ki-lin* appeared before China's most important people as a blessing from the gods and could be seen only by those with great virtue and wisdom.

In the sixth century B.C., however, *Ki-lin* was just a haunting memory. For hundreds of years, China's various states had been at war with one another. Chinese leaders did not help their suffering people, and no one saw the wondrous unicorn.

During this difficult time, a sweet, honorable woman lived by the base of a sacred mountain. She was wise and devout but very sad as she had no son.

The Chinese people believe that to be without a son is cause for the deepest grief. Only the oldest son can worship at each family's home altar, praying to the family's ancestors. Only the son's prayer, they say, keeps the ancestors' spirits alive.

Every household in China—from the most luxurious palace to the most humble hut—has an altar. Burning candles scented with powdered wood keeps away the darkness demons. Above the candles are hung the beautifully carved wooden tablets used for spirit worship. The spirits of Chinese ancestors govern and guide their descendents' everyday lives, while their children provide hope for the future.

Desperate for a son, the good Chinese woman made a pilgrimage to a holy temple on top of the sacred mountain. She planned to plead with the gods one final time. Traveling in a most favorable wind as she climbed the rocky path up the mountain, she stepped into the footprint of the magical *Ki-lin*.

Suddenly, a beautiful unicorn stood before her. The *Ki-lin* bowed, kneeling down to drop from his mouth a piece of jade. This most precious stone of China is a gem of magic, empowering owners and bringing them good fortune. The milky green stone lay before the woman's tired feet. She picked up the cool, smooth rock and read the tiny carving on one side:

Thy son shall be a ruler without a throne.

The *Ki-lin* vanished at once, but the woman held on to her gift. Although the world's jade supply had long come from the mountains of China, the woman knew her stone was special, a blessing from the gods. So when she later gave birth to a son, she expected greatness.

Named *Kung Fu Tzu*, or Confucius, the boy was unusually wise. He became one of China's most influential leaders, a philosopher instead of an emperor. His teachings helped the Chinese to live better, more morally and with less warring. He ruled without a throne, and his ideas remain vital today, over two thousand years after his death.

The writings of Confucius have long been memorized by Chinese schoolchildren. The Confucian philosophy encompasses respect for nature, one's ancestors, and the continuity of life after death.

The story of *Ki-lin* is the ancient Chinese legend of Confucius's birth. In modern-day China, the unicorn is still regarded as a powerful omen of goodness. If a family has an extraordinarily bright son, he is called "son of the unicorn" or "gift of the unicorn," a blessing from the gods.

Confucius

Let the Prince be prince, the minister minister,
the father father, and the son son.

—Confucius

n the middle of the first month of the Chinese New Year, the Feast of the Lanterns is celebrated throughout China. Vendors sell colorful paper lanterns, some painted with a boy riding on a unicorn. When you give such a lantern as a gift to a friend, you are saying: "I wish that you might have a very bright son."

In 1860, just such a son was born. With his glittering black eyes and sun-colored skin, the baby was a blessing to his family and their ancestors. His joyous parents named him *Gim Gong*, which means "double brilliance." The Lues (in China, the last name is written first) could see that their boy was gifted, extremely intelligent, and sensitive to the natural world around him.

The village where Gim Gong grew up was a small farming community not far from Canton. Located in the southern part of China, Lung On enjoyed a warm, subtropical climate where produce flourished and the branches of blossoming fruit trees held up the sun like a sweet orange. The Lue family worked together in their fields and gardens, growing the food they needed and selling the extra at market. Lady Moon shone down on them like a great white lantern.

Gim Gong's mother had found a packet of sweet orange seeds tucked into her wedding trunk, a gift from her own mother. Fruit was as good as gold coins to the Chinese farmers. So she planted the seeds and made cuttings, grafting and then replanting. Gim Gong's mother patiently experimented with her beloved orange trees and, after seven years, her harvest was wildly abundant. Huge, delicious oranges weighed down the branches in Gim Gong's yard.

Gim Gong spent much time in his mother's kitchen-garden, where she grew the family's food. He had been banished from the family's rice paddies after he fell in the watery fields and almost died. Gim Gong's mother showed the boy how to use a small, soft brush for transferring pollen from one tree to another, cross-pollinating from one variety of fruit to a slightly different variety. When he stood in the orange grove in the hazy light of a full moon, Gim Gong watched his mother's small back bent over her seedlings, tending. Gradually, his night vision narrowed until the boy became the little trees, their shoots, their roots, part of the world at the tips of his mother's calloused, moonlit fingers.

Water takes whatever shape it can; wind passes along the surfaces of things. Young Gim Gong began to experiment on his own. He used the black mud from birds' nests as planting soil and slid cool seeds under his father's hens to try to warm them. He planted flowers next to the produce, growing white lilies with purple cabbages in a single plot. Gim Gong talked out loud to his plants, encouraging the flowering of vines and giving thanks for the magical bloom of a well-loved garden.

School was a much less pleasant place for young Gim Gong. He was a good student, a quick learner. But he was smarter than most of his teachers, and his schoolmates teased him for playing with flowers and nursing wounded birds. So the boy preferred to learn on his own, to listen to the wisdom of his garden and feel the soft earth beneath his small, sturdy feet.

garden

When wings are grown.
birds and children fly away.

—*Chinese proverb*

When Gim Gong was around twelve years old, the Lue family celebrated the return of the boy's uncle with great excitement. In those days, very few Chinese people traveled outside their own country. But an increasing number of young men were hiring themselves out as laborers, trading years of hard work for passage to other countries.

Gim Gong's uncle worked in "Gold Mountain," as the Chinese people then called the United States. In California, gold had been discovered. The Chinese villagers talked of the haunted "ghost world" across the sea, where "ghost men" lifted treasures from the earth. America fascinated and frightened them. Gim Gong's uncle became the center of attention for weeks.

Gim Gong's view of the world was dramatically altered by his uncle's strange stories of life among the "foreign ghosts," the white-skinned people of America. The boy wanted to smell the salty ocean. He longed to explore a faraway land brimming with unfamiliar birds and plants. He dreamed of meeting the American ghosts with their short light hair, tight clothes, and wide eyes.

In the spring of 1872, Gim Gong and a half dozen older boys boarded a small boat with square, colored sails called a *sampan*. The boys traveled in a favorable wind, sailing almost a hundred miles downriver to the bustling city of Hong Kong. Gim Gong carried a sack of fat, sweet oranges from his mother's garden.

For the next two moons, the Chinese boys lived in dank, dark berths on a ship to America. Gim Gong was constantly seasick, so he lay quietly, daydreaming and fondling the little red bag his mother had sewn for him. Before he had left Lung On, his mother had burned incense, tucking the ashes into a small bag and tying it around Gim Gong's neck. She had prayed to the Thunder God for favorable winds for her young son's safe passage. Her prayers were answered.

Gum San, the Land of the Golden Mountain, was thick with foreign ghosts when Gim Gong landed in San Francisco. Fortunately, a Chinatown had been created there, a haven for the Chinese, with specialty shops catering to the thousands of Asian immigrants. In 1869, more than six thousand Chinese workers had arrived in California to help build the railroad all the way to the East Coast. Many workers died. The survivors, and the waves of

sampan

Chinese immigrants that followed, lived together in the Chinatowns they formed on both coasts.

The foreign ghosts called Gim Gong "Lue" (pronounced *Loo-ee*). This pleased him because the Chinese boy had quickly decided that he wanted to be an American, too.

But Lue did not look anything like the foreign ghosts. His hair, for example, was braided in a very long queue. (Pronounced like the letter Q, the word is French for "tail.") Lue's queue hung down his back like a snake, winding almost to his knees. He wore loose cotton trousers and a matching jacket of black calico with shiny brass buttons. His thick-soled shoes were made out of cloth. His small eyes were almond shaped. His skin was brownish.

Lue found steady work in a shoe factory, where he was paid a dollar a day. Unlike the other boys with whom he had immigrated, Lue's travel fees had been paid for by his uncle. Since he was not indentured, Lue was able to send money home for his family to use in the ongoing expansion of their land holdings. This was a great honor for the Lues, and for their young son.

Some moons after his factory job began, Lue heard about a better-paying job at the C. T. Sampson Shoe Factory in North Adams, a small town in western Massachusetts. The ambitious boy applied for the position.

Like the fifty other Chinese workers who arrived with him at the train station in North Adams, Lue was unaware that they had been hired to break a workers' strike. The North Adams factory men were angry, some threatening the immigrants' lives. To ensure their safety, the Chinese

long braid (queue)

factory men were housed in barracks at the rear of the old brick building where they worked. Lue's job was in the bottoming room, where he fastened thin soles to shoes made out of leather.

Several church leaders in North Adams organized a Sunday School for the Chinese workers. Volunteers from the various churches in town met with the young foreigners in the factory dormitory, teaching them English and religion. At that time, Chinese people were either Buddhist, Taoist, or Confucianist. The Americans hoped to convert all the immigrants to Christianity.

Fanny Amelia Burlingame was an enthusiastic volunteer teacher at the Sampson Shoe Factory. A brilliant woman in her forties, Fanny lived with her widowed father and two unmarried sisters in a big house surrounded by an acre of gardens. She was adept at math and botany and had pledged her allegiance to Jesus Christ. Energetic and craving the intellectual stimulation denied to most women in the late 1800s, Fanny found herself drawn to the keenly intelligent Chinese boy name Lue. She soon appointed herself the boy's private tutor.

Fanny's father was a successful storeowner with a comfortable income and good social standing. His most famous relative was Anson Burlingame, an American ambassador to China. The Burlingame Treaty was a trade bill Anson had negotiated in 1868, establishing freedom for citizens to travel between the U.S. and China. For this reason, the Burlingames were well versed in Chinese history and more supportive than many Americans of the rights of Chinese immigrants. Still, the liberal

Fannie Burlingame and relatives (Fanny is on the far left)

Burlingames were a product of their time, unable to view Chinese Americans as equals in a society that exalted white men above all others.

As he learned to speak, read, and write in English, Lue gradually discarded his Chinese farm boy customs. He cut off his queue, wore tailored shirts and woolen pants, replaced his chopsticks with a knife and fork. Faithfully attending church services at the Burlingames' Baptist parish, Lue became fascinated with Bible stories and the Christian martyr Jesus. Eventually, he converted to Christianity and was baptized. For the rest of his life, Lue prayed to the Christian God while upholding the values of Confucianism.

The Burlingames lived in a ten-room brick house with wide porches, a barn, lots of fertile land, and a greenhouse.

Baptist Church, North Adams, where Lue Gim Gong was baptized

Lue loved to visit "Mother Fanny," as he called his tutor, spending long Sunday afternoons in the Burlingames' gardens. He marveled at the exotic plants that thrived in the hothouse, blooming all year round. He liked to surround himself with the fragrance and splurge of abundant plant life. In the spring, Lue would wander along the winding dirt paths that led to the wildflower beds, rampant rose bushes, and snow apple trees full of songbirds.

As his grasp of the language improved, Lue began to share with Mother Fanny the plant wisdom he had brought from China. She was intrigued with Lue's ideas about cross-pollination and convinced her father to put the young Chinese boy to work in the family's gardens.

Although he was unaware of his good fortune, Lue Gim Gong had stepped in the footprint of *Ki-lin*. He had been blessed with a sponsor. For the rest of her life, Fanny Burlingame would encourage and support Lue Gim Gong in his plant wizardry.

Burlingame house in North Adams

unicorn

A teacher can open the door, but the pupil
must go through by himself.

—Chinese proverb

While living and working at the C. T. Sampson Shoe Factory, Lue spent his study time in the little schoolhouse Fanny's father had built for her to tutor local college-bound students. Fanny was not a healthy person, suffering frequent respiratory ailments and long periods confined to her bed. Whenever his tutor was unavailable, too sick or busy teaching others, Lue quietly went to work aiding Mr. Burlingame and Fanny's sisters in their lush gardens and flourishing hothouse.

Fanny's favorite uncle, with whom she had studied as a child, was the author of a reference book on native plants of the South. Over the years, Fanny had continued her studies to become an amateur botanist. So Mother Fanny enthusiastically assisted Lue in planning out a number of experiments he wished to conduct on the Burlingames' vast array of subtropical flora. They spent much time speaking the language of fruit.

When Fanny was healthy, the two companions went on lengthy walks, collecting cuttings and digging up wild roots to be transplanted in the greenhouse. They waited together as seeds fattened in the rich black soil. Lue devised a nontoxic mixture using wood ash that success- fully drove away (but did not kill) pesky insects. He ger- minated vegetable seeds for early harvesting. He nursed droopy plants of all kinds back to radiant health in a corner of the hothouse Fanny dubbed "Lue's sanitarium." He watched the sun pry open tiny buds.

With Mother Fanny's supervision, Lue cross-polli- nated. He then harvested the seeds, planting and carefully tending to the resulting seedlings. Consulting troves of thick botany books from Europe and relying on his own intuitive affinity for the natural world, Lue conducted magic in the Burlingames' gardens. The air ripened with blossoms and new fruit. Mother Fanny was as enthralled as her gifted student with the marvels that resulted from their experiments.

According to Fanny Burlingame's niece Julia Plumb, the two researchers successfully cultivated a pear tree that offered sickle pears one year, Bartlett pears the next; the "Famous Beauty," an apple that ripened unseasonably early and was strikingly rich in meat and juice; the "salmonberry," a sweet pink variety of early-ripening rasp-

CROSS-POLLINATION

To cross-pollinate plants, some of the pollen is removed from the stamens of one variety, then dusted onto the pistils of a second, slightly different variety. This second plant is screened over to prevent further pollination by insects or birds. When the plant bears fruit, the seeds are harvested and planted. The new plants will bear fruit that is different from the fruit of both of the "parent" plants.

Cross-pollination creates plants that are superior to the self-fertilized varieties, hardier plants that bear more fruit. This is why horticulturists constantly experiment, making new generations of better plants for ever-improved varieties of fruits, vegetables, and flowers.

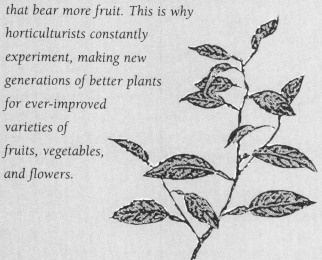

berry; grape-sized red currants called "cherry currants"; and an oversized white currant.

Lue regarded his plants as his special friends, patiently responding to each seedling's individual requirements. He did not need to maintain any written records of his experimentation, memorizing the plants' management programs as a devoted parent would remember each of his or her child's needs. For Lue, this was a time in his life when the sky held more butterflies, fewer rain clouds.

During the mid-1870s, the United States began to slide into an economic depression. Along with much of the American work force, Lue was devastated when his meager wages were sharply reduced and his hours at the factory cut back. Determined to help Lue continue to send money to his family in China, Fanny convinced her father to allow her young friend to move into their home so that they could feed, house, and clothe the struggling immigrant boy.

By 1877, Lue was living like the model American citizen. He labored hard. He was a devout Christian. He spoke English quite fluently, enjoying dinnertime conversations with the American family that had taken him in. He was literate, reading voraciously and taking classes like mechanical engineering. He believed in democracy and freedom.

Some of Lue's Chinese friends regarded these lifestyle choices as proof of betrayal. His peers scolded him for his ambitions, his aspirations for acceptance into white society. Lue Gim Gong was not a "foreign ghost " but, his friends complained, he was pretending to be something he was not. Lue Gim Gong slept in a soft ghost bed, wore binding ghost clothes, ate tasteless ghost food. Members of the small Chinese society in North Adams turned their backs on Lue. They scorned and shunned him.

月

亮

moon

Oh eggs, never fight with stones.

—Chinese proverb

H is factory hours reduced to next to nothing, Lue lived and worked at the Burlingames', tending the gardens and serving the family like a houseboy. His status was unclear: Was the young Chinese man a visiting scholar, household help, or an adopted son? His food and lodging were free, but Lue had no earnings to send home to Lung On. He wrote, promising to send money later. The Lues prayed to Gwoon Yum, the Goddess of Mercy, and continued their farm work.

After Fanny's father suffered a stroke, Lue cared for Mr. Burlingame until his death. Then Lue's own health began to deteriorate. He coughed until his lungs bled.

Not yet thirty, Lue lay in his ghost bed waiting for death to take him to his ancestors. The moon hung in the sky outside his bedroom window, a lotus floating in the darkness.

31

Diagnosed with what they used to call consumption, Lue had tuberculosis at a time when the disease often proved fatal. These days, TB can be successfully treated with medication. In 1886, before the invention of antibiotics, Lue was advised to walk up hills backwards as a cure. But he was too weak to even climb out of bed. The medical specialist Fanny consulted pronounced Lue a hopeless case. He would be dead before the year ended. Lue Gim Gong felt like fire wrapped in paper. Death had planted itself, but he hung on to his belief in the magical power of spring.

Prescriptions and treatments proved useless, and Lue's illness worsened. Lady Moon did not smile on him, and the cold picked at his bones. In a final attempt to save Lue's life, Fanny sent him home to China. She hoped that the warm climate there, his mother's healing hands, and secret medicinal herbs might accomplish what she—and Christian prayer and modern medicine—could not.

Lady Moon held the sea in place under the hoards of stars. On this trip, the Pacific was a black pearl, the winds most favorable. Instead of huddling in a small berth below decks, Lue rested comfortably in a spacious steamer stateroom. The sea air helped his labored breathing. As the moon slimmed and faded, Lue began to recover his health.

On August 20, 1886, the *City of New York* steamed into Hong Kong's harbor. Lue traveled by *sampan* to Canton, where family members waited to escort him back to Lung On.

This time, Lue was the center of the village's attention. He coughed blood while regaling his relatives with incredible stories about the foreign ghosts. His mother fed him soups, ancient healing mixtures she prepared after counsel from the local medicine shop's herbalists. Lue's strength returned, the "spitting-blood disease" cured.

While living with the Burlingames in North Adams, Lue had slept in his own room, on a soft mattress between cool linen sheets. He padded barefoot across the warm, wool carpet to his mahogany desk, where he wrote in a leather-bound journal under the yellow glow of a brass lamp.

In Lung On, Lue slept on the floor in a crowded room shared with other family members: no bed, no sheets, no carpet, no desk, no journal. During the day, he helped his mother in the family's orange grove. Once again he toiled within the boundaries of the garden, speaking the language of fruit. His family, however, no longer understood their Gim Gong and his strange talk of earth science and Christ the Savior.

With his shorn hair and odd Christian ideas, Lue Gim Gong was quickly ostracized by the villagers of Lung On. Some believed the young man was possessed by a foreign ghost, a white ghost that had taken over his mind and body. They asked for protection from their gods, scattering flowers and burning incense. Once again, Lue's peers turned their backs, scorning and shunning him.

When the air was full of the vapors of dawn, his family still sleeping around him, Lue wrote desperate letters to Mother Fanny. Devoted as ever, she quickly devised a plan to once again help her young friend.

America had enacted an exclusion policy to keep

Chinese immigrants from entering the country and com-
peting with U.S. citizens for jobs. Chinese Americans living in the U.S. were mistreated, blamed for labor short-
ages, their stores and restaurants boycotted. This wave of
prejudice, called the "Yellow Peril," continued until 1943,
when the cruel, discriminating laws were finally revoked.
Until then, entry to the U.S. was allowed only for certain
Chinese visitors such as students, teachers, diplomats, and
merchants.

Fanny sent Lue some money to purchase curios from
Hong Kong for sale in the U.S. She advised him to buy passage to America under the guise of a Chinese merchant.
She also provided the funds he would need for his passage
back to Massachusetts.

In the same moon, Lue's mother consulted a respect-
ed matchmaker, seeking a bride for her twenty-six-year-old
son. If Gim Gong could marry well and sire a son, the
family believed, he would be happy living in China—and
most important, his spirit would be prayed for after death.
Lue was confused. He understood only that Lady Moon's
tides drew him back to a distant shore.

Following Chinese custom, Lue's family purchased
from her family the young girl selected by the matchmaker. Now regarded by her society as the Lue family's
property, Gim Gong's wife-to-be would live with and work
for them for the rest of her life.

The sun shone, the moon reflected, but the bride-to-
be would never marry Lue Gim Gong.

On the morning of his wedding day, Lue ran away
from his betrothed, leaving behind forever his Chinese

home and family, his life in Lung On. He fled on foot, then on a steamer, disguised as a merchant with products for the American market. Lue would never again return to China. And Lue Gim Gong's family would never forgive him for the public shame and dishonor his startling disappearance created for them.

bride-to-be

月

亮

moon

To forget one's ancestors is to be a tree without roots.

—Chinese proverb

Crossing the black ocean for the third time, Lue felt like a lantern, alight, full of beauty and wind. En route to Mother Fanny's, he received a telegram from her sister Cynthia's new husband, Major William Dumville: "Proceed by train to Sanford, Florida. We will meet you there. Have bought grove in DeLand."

According to Cynthia Burlingame Dumville, "The cordiality of the people is DeLand's chief charm." Of course, she was white-skinned and moneyed. Her peers, the wealthier set from North Adams, were building summer homes in DeLand, a small town in central Florida where stately oaks draped with Spanish moss stood next to tropical cabbage palms.

C. T. Sampson, the owner of the shoe factory where Lue once worked, summered in DeLand. Dressed in crisp, white linen suits, men like Mr. Sampson and Major Dumville were invited by DeLand's upper-class society for oyster roasts and games of croquet on vast green lawns.

The only Chinese person in town and the first Asian most of the populace had seen, Lue faced a kind of racism he had never before encountered: subtle, Southern-style bigotry. Eyebrows lifted and conversations halted when the newcomer approached. No party invitations for the Chinaman. No hearty welcomes from the town's churches. No one even offered him a frosty glass of iced tea on a humid afternoon. Called "colored" behind his back, Lue was branded an outsider and kept at a polite but firm distance.

Since the society people of DeLand would have deemed it truly scandalous, Lue could no longer share living quarters with the Burlingame sisters. Instead, Fanny set him up in a small, two-room shack some fifty yards away from the two-story, white clapboard home she shared with Major and Mrs. Dumville. Lue still ate his meals with Mother Fanny, and he sat with her out on the wisteria-covered front porch. But Lue spent most of his time tending to Major Dumville, who was ill with a nervous disorder called palsy, or working in the Major's garden and grove.

In order to populate the small town bearing his name, founder Henry A. DeLand lured Northerners with an enticing "free ride" to Florida. He promised that orange groves would thrive in the mild climate—or he would repay growers for any failed investments in citrus. Major Dumville had decided to take advantage of Mr. DeLand's unusual offer, as had many other risk-takers willing to put

Burlingame house in DeLand

roots down in central Florida for at least a few seasons. The Northern transplants cross-bred their dreams in the Southern citrus groves, hoping the trees would drop golden fruits like coins into their outstretched palms.

Using nature's bounty rather than store-bought fertilizers and tools, Lue prepared the sandy Florida soil with nutrient-rich garden compost from leaves, grass cuttings, and barnyard waste. Implanting the soil with tobacco stems added more nutrients and cleared out the insects. Lue carefully picked at the sandy clay, tilling out the lime rock, enriching the Florida dirt to support the life he would plant there. Soon, pink camellias blossomed beside azaleas and crepe myrtles, white magnolias next to jasmine, hollies, and honeysuckle. Orange blossoms wafted their sweet scent.

Lue had grown a bushy mustache during his escape from China. His jet hair was speckled with gray. His past haunted him, a phantom presence he could neither escape nor embrace. He did not even attempt to sell the curios he had brought back in his guise as a merchant. To comfort her "son" and ensure his stability, Fanny applied for and secured U.S. citizenship for Lue Gim Gong in 1887.

Lue was quieter now, more introverted, deeply saddened by the loss of his family and humbled by his own disrespectful actions. Nature comforted him, and he felt the same intimacy with the flora of Florida as he had enjoyed in North Adams and Lung On.

It was in DeLand, however, that Lue Gim Gong would reveal his plant wizardry to the rest of America. And it was his genius with citrus fruit that would make him world famous and revolutionize the Florida orange industry.

genius

The young should inspire us with respect.
How do we know
that their future will not equal our present?
But if a man
has reached forty or fifty without being heard of,
he indeed is incapable of commanding respect.

—Confucius

Lue had developed a theory about the orange trees growing in central Florida. After studying weather trends in the state, Lue realized that the winters there were becoming colder. He knew that this dramatic and dangerous change was due to the ongoing destruction of the tall pine forests of northern Florida, where land was being rapidly developed for housing and razed for acres of citrus groves. Cold winter air was blowing farther south, no longer blocked by thickets of evergreens. Lue predicted that central Florida would begin to experience longer, colder winter seasons. DeLand, he said, would soon suffer winter freezes, days when the temperature would fall below 32°F. This is the kind of cold that

43

kills citrus trees. In his mind's eye, Lue could foresee acres
of threadbare groves, iced trees glistening in death.

No one in DeLand believed Lue's theory. The farmers
and growers laughed at his predictions. Frosts were rare in
that Southern town, and there had been only one freeze
that anyone could remember. Freezes in central Florida,
the townspeople insisted, were practically impossible.
Blind to the fact that overdevelopment was building into a
catastrophic force, the citizens of DeLand dismissed Lue
Gim Gong.

But Lue Gim Gong had stepped in the footprint of the
magical *Ki-lin*. And he gave birth to a miraculous idea: he
would develop a hardy orange, a variety of citrus fruit that
could survive the coldest weather. He would experiment,
cross-pollinating and transplanting until he had created
the first frost-resistant orange.

freeze

The wise man listens to his own mind:
the foolish man heeds the mob.

—Chinese proverb

nly Mother Fanny encouraged her friend's wild genius. But one supporter was enough. Lue embarked on his project. He cross-pollinated, using two of the most vigorous citrus varieties in their grove: a Hart's Late, a standard orange that ripens late in the citrus season; and a juicy orange called the Mediterranean Sweet. Then Lue tended to his new plant very carefully. The little seeds demanded much of him, and Lue bowed to their needs, bent before his gems as if polishing precious jade.

From the healthy Late/Sweet tree he had created and nurtured, Lue selected a single fat, sweet orange. He removed eighteen seeds and planted them. When twelve seedlings popped up, Lue transplanted them by grafting the best buds onto the roots of older trees, embedding the

Lue Gim Gong in his wagon in the DeLand groves
(Mother Fanny wears the long checkered apron)

buds from the seedlings into slits made in the older trees' roots. This method speeds up growth. Within one to two years the seedlings can bear fruit, rather than taking the full seven years a non-grafted citrus tree requires for reaching maturity. Lue wrapped his seedlings with waxed cloth to protect them from wind, heat, and cold, and he waited patiently for new shoots to appear on the old tree roots.

Fall faded away with the clamorous chirping of the cicadas, and winter shoved in like a fist. Dead wood snapped underfoot, the earth hardening overnight. In December 1894, then again in February 1895, central Florida was battered by severely cold weather. The second frost, which caused the temperature to drop and hover around 20° F for three days, was the worst freeze in Florida's recorded history. It is still referred to there as the Big Freeze. Fish died, frozen in place in the iced lakes. Vegetable crops were flash-frozen in the rock-hard soil. Citrus trees died by the acre, icicle branches heavy with blackened fruit.

Devastated, farmers dug trenches in their fields, burying millions of destroyed oranges, grapefruit, and tangerines. The sky over Florida turned gray with the smoke of burning citrus, the growers forced to rid their groves of thousands of dead trees. Ninety-five percent of Florida's citrus groves were wiped out. Children went hungry that year, their families unable to recover from the agricultural losses caused by the unexpected cold.

When the morning sun had sucked up the frost, Lue wept as he stepped gingerly on crunchy black fruit, his grove a graveyard haunted by the skeletons of hundreds of dead trees. Lue's cross-bred seedlings, however, managed to survive the cold, hardy as predicted.

The storm clouds hurried off, as clouds do in the Florida sky. Fueled with hope, Lue continued to tend to his experimental orange stock. He removed the healthy shoots, transplanting them at the end of the citrus growing season. Then Lue waited to see the new variety of citrus tree he had invented.

After the Big Freeze, Fanny's health deteriorated markedly and she coughed constantly. She hired a maid-companion, a twenty-year-old girl from nearby Pierson, a Swedish colony of immigrants with big families and white-blonde hair. Red-cheeked and blue-eyed, pretty LaGette Hagstrom comforted and cheered Fanny and Lue for the next seven years.

Lue's other favored companions were two Arabian horses, a mare and her foal. Baby trotted beside her mother, both horses following Lue around like pet dogs. One would pull Lue in his rickety yellow carriage, transporting boxes of oranges to the packinghouse beyond the groves. Located near the street, the packinghouse had wide doors and smelled of ripe fruit. Horse-drawn wagons would come regularly to load up the boxed produce, carting it away to the local railroad station to ship north to markets.

Lue, Fanny, and LaGette traveled north every spring, taking steamers up the St. Johns and Mississippi Rivers, then long train rides to get to Massachusetts. There they escaped the intolerable heat and humidity of Florida, spending the warmest months in the Burlingames' home.

Houses in DeLand did not have air conditioning (which had yet to be invented), so the summer heat there was thick and uncomfortable.

Lue continued his work in the gardens and greenhouse in North Adams. He developed a superior tomato plant that grew fat fruit in clusters on a vine as long as fifteen feet. He grew peaches that ripened as late as Thanksgiving. With Mother Fanny's help, Lue marketed some of his plant inventions, selling seeds in the catalog of a national agriculture company. Some days, he could smell a future coming that was as sweet as mowed grass, spills of catalpa, and night-blooming jasmine.

Newspapers and magazines across the U.S. began to run stories on Lue Gim Gong's marvelous plants: the salmon raspberry, the late-ripening apple and peach, the cherry currant, the clustering tomato. Articles described a perfumed grapefruit he had cultivated with sweet-smelling fruit that measured as big as twenty-one inches in diameter. Lue even developed crystallized candy and grapefruit pickles made from the thick, clean-smelling skin of his prize-sized fruit.

The plant wizard's most widely recognized creation, however, was his winter-hardy orange. Even the most cynical people in DeLand were forced to admit that Lue Gim Gong's oranges were bigger, more beautiful, tastier, and *much* longer lasting. In fact, Lue's special oranges could remain on the tree for as long as three *years*—and still taste delicious!

Lue's special variety of orange was indeed cold resistant. The frigid winters that continued to plague DeLand

Selecting Ripe Oranges and Grapefruit in Lue Gim Gong's Citrus Groves, DeLand, Florida.

LUE GIM GONG'S CITRUS GROVES

**Oranges, Grapefruit, Tangerines, Mandarins, Satsumas, Lemons, Etc.
And the "Lue Gim Gong," An All Year-Round Orange and
Grapefruit. Shipped From DeLand, Florida.**

We spare no expense to make this fruit good. It is not picked from the trees indiscriminately, but is selected according to ripeness. Every orange is examined and wiped or brushed to remove dirt or other impurities, and they are carefully graded before sizing. The fruit in each box is of uniform size and wrapped in Hammerschlag waxed paper, such as is used for wrapping butter and candy. We have used this paper since 1889, and find that it tends to preserve the fruit and also to prevent those which are decayed from injuring any with which they may come in contact.

Our boxes are made by the W. A. Merryday Co., of Palatka, Fla., especially for us—are extra heavy and of the best quality and make.

No job or contract packing. This fruit not to be sold on condition but on its merits, and guaranteed to be good when received. As we would not wish to buy decayed fruit, neither do we sell it. "Therefore all things whatsoever ye would that men should do to you, do ye even so to them, for this is the law and the prophets." Matt. 7:12, and found in the teachings of Confucius. This is not my preaching but my practice in all things all my life. "Providing for honest things not only in the sight of the Lord but also in the sight of men." 2 Cor. 8:21. Faults I have, and mistakes I have made, but my intentions and aims are to be honest and honorable in all things or dealings and my will is good to encourage the right and discourage the wrong. If there are more honest and honorable and better ways to do business, even in my declining age, I am willing to learn. If any error address.

LUE GIM GONG

DeLand, Florida, or North Adams, Mass.

*An advertisement for Lue Gim Gong's
citrus, available by mail*

*Lue Gim Gong, Fanny Burlingame, and the Hagstroms
(Lue stands with the horses; Fanny, in the dark dress, stands
on the other side of the horses; LaGette Hagstrom is seated
in the front row, third from left)*

proved that Lue's trees could withstand a good deal of frost, more than any other variety around. The fruit hung happily through the heaviest rains too, ripening much later than other orange varieties. His harvests were uniformly abundant, the big sweet oranges juicy and with few seeds. Lue's oranges shipped well, traveling long distances without spoilage (important in the days before modern refrigeration was available for shipped produce). And since the fruit ripened so late in the season when other kinds of oranges were unavailable, Lue's prime harvest could demand higher prices. Lue's oranges were a delicious success.

When Mother Fanny passed away in 1903, she did not leave a will. For nearly thirty years, she had supported Lue, loving him like the son she never bore. Lue's name had been entered in the Burlingames' family records as Fanny's "adopted" son. But he had worked long hours for the Burlingames, tending to their gardens and groves, and had received no wages. Lue did not own the little house he had lived in for seventeen years. The two groves where his hardy oranges flourished were deeded to the Burlingames. After so many years dependent on Fanny, Lue was left penniless, totally inexperienced in financial matters, grief-stricken and desperate.

LaGette and Lue accompanied Fanny's body on the long, sad trip to North Adams, where she was buried. Lue prayed, then he begged Fanny's sisters to deed him the property in DeLand. Since Cynthia had refused to return south after the death of Major Dumville four years earlier, the sisters agreed. They also paid Lue twelve thousand dollars, back wages for decades of unpaid labor. To show his gratitude, Lue sent crates of his best citrus to the sisters every year after that. And each Memorial Day, he sent them a box full of fragrant boughs of Cape Jasmine for Mother Fanny's grave.

heartbreak

If you are humble, you will not be laughed at;
if you are diligent, you will be successful;
if you are gracious, you will get along well
with others.

—Confucius

When they returned to DeLand, Lue spent four thousand dollars on land, increasing his holdings to a total of one hundred fifteen acres. Racism was far stronger than brotherly love in early Florida, however, and Christian Southerners cringed at the Chinaman's wealth. "Colored" people were not supposed to be prosperous in the turn-of-the-century South, so the townsfolk treated Lue with even more contempt than before. He stopped attending services at the Baptist church and rarely traveled into town. Like a sturdy tree, Lue remained rooted in his own grove, bending only to the earth as the wind demanded.

To illustrate their disapproval of his prosperity, some influential city residents discouraged local orange grove laborers from working for Lue Gim Gong. Left without assistance at harvest time, Lue turned to his Swedish friends, the Hagstroms. LaGette's large family pitched in, picking the luscious fruit and packing box after box for shipping.

Unfortunately, the Hagstroms also judged their tea by its color, not its scent. Despite their own problems as immigrants, the Swedes disapproved of crossbred cultures. So when Lue asked LaGette's father for his daughter's hand in marriage, the answer was a resounding, painful, decidedly prejudiced *no*.

Heartbroken and wretchedly lonely, Lue ached through the long, humid nights. Lady Moon looked down, stern, unsmiling. Lue sent money and apologetic letters to his family in China. No one responded. More isolated than ever before, Lue buried himself in his experiments in his gardens and groves.

Articles published in horticulture journals at the time increasingly took note of Lue Gim Gong's research. Widely praised by the scientific community, Lue was labeled a "plant wizard" and a "horticultural genius." His year-round orange was hailed as one of the finest commercial varieties of citrus fruit ever grown.

Four years after developing his hardy orange, Lue had cross-pollinated a new variety of grapefruit. A cross between the Florida common grapefruit and the trifoliata, a sturdy orange, Lue's new variety of grapefruit could brave the coldest temperatures. The new type of citrus tree grew only one fruit per branch, rather than many in clusters. This meant that the heavy fruit would not weigh down the tree, allowing for better harvests.

Immediately popular with Florida growers, Lue's hardy grapefruit was saving the citrus industry much money, as were his hardy oranges. In fact, Lue's citrus varieties were also being grown in California and in other parts of the world where fruit harvests were threatened by cold weather. People all over the globe were benefiting from Lue Gim Gong's plant research.

In 1911, the American Pomological Society ("pomological" refers to the science of fruit growing) awarded their highest honor to the "late keeping orange" developed by

Lue inherited the Burlingame house in DeLand

Lue. This was the first time the Wilder Silver Medal had been awarded for citrus. The hardy Florida orange became famous, known worldwide as the "Lue Gim Gong." The medal was not given to Lue, however, but to Glen St. Mary Nurseries, the company in charge of marketing Lue's orange variety.

Despite his blossoming fame, Lue was not making much money from his inventions. He was bewildered by contracts and financial transactions, and he typically gave away buds and fruit to the many visitors who came to see the plant wizard's magical groves. From the seeds and cuttings Lue shared with them, other growers cultivated their own groves of trees, soon heavy with Lue Gim Gong oranges and the late-keeping grapefruit also called Lue Gim Gong. In this way, groves of Lue Gim Gong citrus multiplied in number until tens of thousands of the hardy fruit trees were in bloom.

Since he had long felt unwelcome in the churches of DeLand, Lue created a simple prayer garden at his home. Built beneath the overhanging branches of two big orange trees, the outdoor church was filled with the scent of wild yellow jasmine and Cherokee roses, the sound of mockingbirds singing overhead, the rustle of warm wind slipping through green leaves.

Using orange crates for pews and a crude pulpit, Lue conducted prayer meetings for the visitors who came to see the "Chinese wizard of the orange." He asked his guests to sign a logbook, amassing thousands of signatures each year. Scientists, nature lovers, amateur botanists, and curious tourists from all over the world visited "Florida's

Lue and his horse

wonderful old plant wizard." Tour boats traveling down the St. Johns River made regular stops at Lue's groves. Schoolteachers brought their classes to see Lue's garden and to meet the marvelous citrus genius.

By 1917, Lue Gim Gong was white haired and fragile. He carried his thin body like a fish in a dark, heavy sea. Eating mostly from his own gardens, Lue lived sparsely, dressed in ragged clothes, always tilling the soil. His closest friends were his two horses and a rooster named March. Lue had raised the rooster, nursing it after a hawk dropped the baby bird in his garden. Lue taught March to ride on his shoulder and to catch the table scraps he tossed during meals. March learned to bow his combed head as if in prayer, waiting for bits of corn. When March finally died, Lue stuffed the bird and stationed him by his front door.

Over the years, Lue's income dwindled and his bills piled up. He spent the little money he had on books and horse feed. Since he gave away his trees and mismanaged his earnings, Lue was constantly broke. In his last years, he came close to forfeiting his property because he was unable to pay his mortgage. On two occasions, Lue's admirers donated the funds to save his home and groves when they read of his financial problems in newspapers and horticulture magazines.

Eventually, Lue was too poor and feeble to care for himself and his groves. Lue's cart had tipped over after he drove through a nest of yellow jackets one day, scaring his old horse into a wild trot. Lue depended on a crutch after the accident, hobbling around his overgrown gardens.

Lue Gim Gong and his pet rooster

Lue Gim Gong's barn after his death

Like a paper lantern, tender as wind on a stick, Lue Gim Gong leaned on his crutch, his trees bowing down around him. In his heart, he knew that the life of the citrus tree is longer than the life of a man. He understood that, this time, death had been planted. Body all thorn and bone, hands worn from caring, Lue Gim Gong died on June 3, 1925.

Almost forty years after the Boston doctor told the young Chinese man he had less than one year to live, hundreds of people from all over the world attended the funeral of Lue Gim Gong. Eulogies praised the Chinese-American horticulturist for his courage, his genius, his gentle kindness to plants, animals, nature—and the people who never quite accepted him. That night in Lue Gim Gong's grove, the branches of the orange trees held up Lady Moon like a white China bowl with an offering of jade fruit for the gods.

When Lue's home was packed up, cardboard boxes full of uncashed checks were found stacked in his tumble-down barn. Didn't Lue understand that these checks were worth a lot of money? Was he unable to transport himself to the bank in DeLand, or unwilling to face the unfriendly townspeople he might encounter there?

Lue's reputation as a mysterious eccentric, a wizard with unearthly powers, sprouted and grew wildly. Stories began to spread, crediting him with the development of a pure black rose. Newspapers reported Lue had grown a bush that put forth seventeen different varieties of roses in seven different colors, all from a single root. People talked of the incredible tree he had cultivated that grew oranges, grapefruit, *and* tangerines. It was rumored that the old Chinese man planted when the position of the moon dictated, a secret he had learned from the nature spirits. Some whispered that Lue Gim Gong was counseled by ghosts, his dead ancestors, and the wondrous *Ki-lin.*

Lue's remarkable work with plants was honored in 1933 at the Chicago World's Fair. In 1940, his discoveries were highlighted at the New York World's Fair. But in his adopted hometown of DeLand, Lue remained as overlooked in death as he had been during the decades he had lived there under the moss-hung oaks. His large library was sold off, most of his journals and personal papers destroyed, his grave left unmarked.

In 1930, a historian from New York visiting the Oakdale Cemetery in DeLand was outraged to discover Lue Gim Gong's grave lacked a headstone. He alerted the New York Historical Society, and they raised the funds for a simple grave marker.

Almost seventy years later, a sculptor was commissioned to make a bronze bust of Lue Gim Gong. In 1999, a DeLand philanthropist donated funds to improve his gravesite. The marker was embedded in a huge rose-colored headstone with 24-carat-gold lettering that reads:

Lue Gim Gong,

1860–1929

"The Citrus Wizard"

These days, Lue's research is evident in most varieties of commercial oranges grown in the South, bred to withstand contemporary weather patterns that include annual winter freezes. The Lue Gim Gong orange has gradually been replaced by other varieties, and you can find only a handful of the trees bearing his name. Several Lue Gim Gong orange trees surround the bronze bust of the citrus wizard, which is on display in a museum garden in DeLand. A plaque there and an engraving on Lue's headstone convey the personal motto of the Chinese-American man of double brilliance, Florida's own gift of the unicorn:

> *No one should live in this world for himself alone,*
> *but to do good for those who come after him.*

Lue Gim Gong had no descendents to pray for his spirit. Perhaps the ghost of the citrus wizard haunts DeLand to this day, pouring through the gardens like wind. Maybe Lue still stoops in his grove, gathering lumps of wet earth and small green roots, forever tending, tending to his beloved plants.

Lue Gim Gong in his citrus grove in DeLand (1912)

Here is a tree older than the forest itself:
The years of its life defy reckoning.
Its roots have seen upheavals of hill and valley.
Its leaves have known the changes of
                    wind and frost.
The world laughs at its shoddy exterior
And cares nothing for the fine grain
                    of the wood inside.
Stripped free of flesh and hide.
All that remains is the core of truth.

—Han-shan,
classic Tang Dynasty poet of ancient China

Author's Note
and Acknowledgments

While visiting central Florida during the autumn of 2001, my family took a tour of the Henry A. DeLand House Museum. Wandering behind the historic mansion, we discovered the lovely little Lue Gim Gong Memorial Garden, with its remarkably lifelike bronze bust of Florida's citrus wizard. Intrigued, I decided to research the story of this unusual and influential Floridian.

Everyone at the Robert M. Conrad Educational Research Center offered friendly assistance. Rita Gillis and Bill Dreggors provided reading materials, photographs, educational videos, and any firsthand information they had about the life of Lue Gim Gong.

The staff at the duPont-Ball Library of Stetson University helped me locate information on traditional Chinese culture, including poetry, proverbs, and folktales. I also relied on the extensive research conducted by Ruthanne Lum McCunn, who has written so beautifully about Lue Gim Gong and other important Chinese Americans.

While I am grateful to all of these wonderful people for their input on this project, any mistakes in the factual content of the story of Lue Gim Gong are my own. I have taken poetic liberties to recount the tale of a very private and controversial Chinese American living in early Florida. Thus, *Gift of the Unicorn* is full of mystery and myth—just like the life of Lue Gim Gong.

My thanks also go to Rebecca Swensen, Children's Services, Boca Raton Public Library, who has helped me immeasurably.

Chinese symbols

超度光輝

double brilliance

孔子

Confucius

苑

garden

舢舨

sampan

長辮子

long braid (queue)

unicorn

75

月亮

moon

天才

genius

傷心

heartbreak

準新娘

bride-to-be

freeze

壯固老樹

sturdy old tree

Bibliography

Burland, C. A. *Ancient China*. London: Hilton Educational Publications, 1960.

Chang, Isabelle. *Chinese Fairy Tales*. Barre, MA: Barre Publishers, 1965.

Kendall, Carol, and Yao-wen Li. *Sweet and Sour: Tales from China*. New York: Seabury Press, 1978.

McCunn, Ruthanne Lum. *Chinese American Portraits: Personal Histories 1828–1988*. San Francisco: Chronicle Books, 1988.

McCunn, Ruthanne Lum. *Wooden Fish Songs*. Boston: Beacon Press, 1995.

McPharlin, Paul. *Chinese Love Lyrics from Most Ancient to Modern Times*. Mount Vernon, NY: Peter Pauper Press, 1964.

McPhee, John. *Oranges*. New York: Farrar, Straus & Giroux, 1967.

Murray, Marian. *Plant Wizard: The Life of Lue Gim Gong*. New York: Macmillan, 1970.

Sum Nung Au-Young. *The Rolling Pearl*. New York: March & Greenwood, 1930.

Ware, James R. *The Sayings of Confucius.* New York: New American Library, 1955.

Watson, Burton, ed. *Cold Mountain: 100 Poems by the T'ang Poet Han-shan.* New York: Columbia University Press, 1970.

West Volusia Historical Society. "Lue Gim Gong the Citrus Wizard 1860–1925." (brochure) (April 1999).

Wyndham, Robert. *Tales the People Tell in China.* New York: Julian Messner, 1971.

About the Author

VIRGINIA ARONSON is the author of more than 27 published books. Many of these titles are for young readers, including the biography of another notable Asian-American horticulturist, *Konnichiwa Florida Moon: The Story of George Morikami, Pineapple Pioneer*. Virginia currently resides in Florida with her husband, a writer, and their young son, a budding horticulturist.

If you enjoyed reading this book, here are some other books from Pineapple Press on related topics. Ask your local bookseller for our books. For a complete catalog, write to Pineapple Press, P.O. Box 3889, Sarasota, FL 34230 or call 1-800-PINEAPL (746-3275). Or visit our website at www.pineapplepress.com.

Konnichiwa Florida Moon: The Story of George Morikami, Pineapple Pioneer by Virginia Aronson. Suitable for readers aged 7–10 and part of the Pineapple Press Biography for Young Adults series, this is the story of Sukeji "George" Morikami, who arrived at the Japanese farming colony of Yamato in south Florida in 1906. Though he amassed a fortune through the sale of his pineapples, George remained a humble man throughout his life, living simply and eating the crops he grew himself. Before he died, George donated his priceless land to eventually become the Morikami Museum and Japanese Gardens. ISBN 1-56164-263-0 (hb)

Dinosaurs of the South by Judy Cutchins and Ginny Johnston. Rich with dozens of color photos and original art, this book offers new and exciting information to reveal the lives of dinosaurs in the Southern coastal states. ISBN 1-56164-266-5 (hb)

The Florida Water Story by Peggy Sias Lantz and Wendy A. Hale. Follow a raindrop to the sea. ISBN 1-56164-099-9 (hb)

Giant Predators of the Ancient Seas by Judy Cutchins and Ginny Johnston. Explores how scientists use fossil clues to learn about the lives and habitats of the most exciting sea animals that ever lived. ISBN 1-56164-237-1 (hb)

Ice Age Giants of the South by Judy Cutchins and Ginny Johnston. This book chronicles up-to-date discoveries in the field of archaeology and describes how prehistoric animals looked, how they lived, and what they ate. ISBN 1-56164-195-2 (hb)

The Young Naturalist's Guide to Florida by Peggy Sias Lantz and Wendy A. Hale. This enticing book shows you where and how to look for Florida's most interesting natural features and creatures. ISBN 1-56164-051-4 (pb)